DATE DUE

MAY 2 4	
FEB 0 4 2014	
JAN 2 5 2017	
DISCARD	

THE NHL: HISTORY AND HEROES

NEW YORK RANGERS

MICHAEL E. GOODMAN

THE NHL: HISTORY AND HEROES

Published by Creative Education
P.O. Box 227, Mankato, Minnesota 56002
Creative Education is an imprint of The Creative Company.

DESIGN AND PRODUCTION BY **ZENO DESIGN**

Printed in the United States of America

PHOTOGRAPHS BY Corbis (Bettmann, Gary Hershorn/Reuters, Underwood & Underwood), Getty Images (Bruce Bennett Studio, Scott Cunningham, Melchior DiGiacomo, Mitchell Funk, John Giamundo, Hulton Archive, Jim McIsaac, New York Times Co.), Hockey Hall of Fame (Imperial Oil-Turofsky)

LIBRARY OF CONGRESS CATALOGING-IN-PUBLICATION DATA

Goodman, Michael E.
The story of the New York Rangers / by Michael E. Goodman.
p. cm. — (The NHL: history and heroes)
Includes index
ISBN 978-1-58341-619-8
1. New York Rangers (Hockey team)—History. 2. Hockey teams—United States—History. I. Title. II. Series.

GV848.N43G66 2008
796.962'64097471—dc22   2007022603

First Edition

9 8 7 6 5 4 3 2 1

COVER: Wing Jaromir Jagr

NEW YORK
RANGERS

NEW YORK

WITH THEIR HOME ARENAS FEWER THAN 10 MILES (16 KM) APART, THE NEW YORK RANGERS AND NEW JERSEY DEVILS OF THE NATIONAL HOCKEY LEAGUE HAD AN INTENSE AND LONG-ESTABLISHED RIVALRY. BUT THINGS REACHED A FEVER PITCH AS THE CLUBS FACED OFF IN GAME 7 OF THE 1994 EASTERN CONFERENCE FINALS. THE RANGERS SCORED EARLY AND PROTECTED A 1–0 LEAD INTO THE GAME'S FINAL MINUTE. BUT DEVILS WING VALERI ZELEPUKIN THEN QUIETED THE MADISON SQUARE GARDEN CROWD BY SLIPPING A SHOT PAST RANGERS GOALIE MIKE RICHTER TO TIE THE CONTEST. THE CLUBS BATTLED THROUGH

RANGERS

ONE NERVE-RACKING, SUDDEN-DEATH OVERTIME PERIOD AND INTO A SECOND BEFORE THE DEVILS MADE A MISTAKE. RANGERS WING STEPHANE MATTEAU INTERCEPTED A WEAK CLEARING PASS, SKATED AROUND THE DEVILS' NET, AND EDGED A WRAPAROUND SHOT THROUGH THE PADS OF DEVILS GOALIE MARTIN BRODEUR FOR THE GAME WINNER. THE VICTORY PROPELLED THE RANGERS INTO THE STANLEY CUP FINALS AND WITHIN REACH OF THEIR FIRST WORLD CHAMPIONSHIP IN 54 YEARS.

TEX'S RANGERS

IN 1624, DUTCH SETTLERS SEEKING RELIGIOUS freedom crossed the Atlantic Ocean and set up a colony they called New Amsterdam halfway between the British colonies of Massachusetts and Virginia. New Amsterdam didn't stay in Dutch hands for very long, however. In 1664, it was surrendered to the British, who renamed it New York in honor of the king's brother, the duke of York. Despite the change of control, New York retained some of its Dutch heritage in names of places, such as Harlem (originally Haarlem) and Brooklyn (originally Breuckelen), and names of families, such as Roosevelt and Vanderbilt. Dutch settlers also imported one of their games, called *kolven*, which was played on a frozen pond with golf-club-like sticks, a ball, and posts stuck in the ice. It was a forerunner of modern ice hockey, but without the skates.

Nicknamed "The City That Never Sleeps," New York is bustling with traffic, business, and entertainment at all hours of the day and night.

Nearly 300 years later, professional ice hockey officially arrived in New York, thanks to the efforts of sports promoter George Lewis ("Tex") Rickard. In 1925, Rickard helped finance a new sports arena, called Madison Square Garden, located on the city's west side, and needed attractions to fill the arena. He rented out space to a new National Hockey League (NHL) expansion team called the New York Americans ("Amerks" for short), which filled the seats for its games during the 1925–26 season. The following season, Rickard raised $50,000 to purchase his own NHL expansion team and placed it in the Garden along with the Amerks. (The two teams shared arena space until the Amerks went out of business in 1942.)

Rickard's new team didn't have a name yet, but sportswriters began calling it "Tex's Rangers"—a play on words—and the name stuck. They were also nicknamed the "Blueshirts" for the color of their home sweaters. Rickard hired

Jean Ratelle CENTER

Joseph Gilbert Yvonne "Jean" Ratelle demonstrated both skill and dignity on the ice. Teaming with Rod Gilbert and Vic Hadfield on the Rangers' famous "GAG (goal-a-game) Line" during the 1970s, Ratelle consistently ranked among the league's top scorers, topping the 70-point mark 12 times during his career. He was a smooth offensive player who almost never lost his cool during a game. In 1971–72, for example, Ratelle finished third in the league in scoring while being whistled for only two minor penalties all year. Following the season, his peers chose him to receive the Lester Pearson Award as the league's top player.

RANGERS SEASONS: 1960–76
HEIGHT: 6-1 (185 cm)
WEIGHT: 175 (79 kg)

- 776 career assists
- 2-time Lady Byng Trophy winner (as best sportsman)
- 5-time All-Star
- Hockey Hall of Fame inductee (1985)

Madison Square Garden, pictured here in 1925, hosted Rangers games, circuses, and boxing matches until 1967, when a new version was built.

a hockey expert from Toronto named Conn Smythe to organize the Rangers, and Smythe quickly assembled the nucleus of a powerful squad by signing brothers Bill and Bun Cook to play right and left wing, center Frank Boucher, defensemen Ivan "Ching" Johnson and Clarence "Taffy" Abel, and goaltender Lorne Chabot. Before Smythe could direct his team's first NHL game, however, he was fired after an argument with Rickard over player signings and was replaced as coach by Lester Patrick.

On November 16, 1926, Patrick's Rangers made their debut before 13,000 fans at Madison Square Garden and earned a hard-fought, 1–0 victory over the Montreal Maroons. The Blueshirts would go on to top the NHL's American Division that year with a 25–13–6 record, led by Bill Cook, who won the league scoring title with 37 points (33 goals and 4 assists).

The Rangers were an immediate hit in New York, attracting large crowds that often included celebrities dressed in fancy evening wear. Rangers games even started at 8:30 P.M., the same time that curtains went up in nearby Broadway theaters. Commenting on the Rangers' playing ability and style of their audiences, one sportswriter noted, "They were the classiest team in hockey."

A Perfect Gentleman

WHEN THE RANGERS' FIRST COACH, CONN Smythe, was constructing the team's first roster, winger Bill Cook suggested signing a young playmaker from the Western Canada Hockey League named Frank Boucher to be the team's starting center. Smythe made the offer to Boucher even before he met him. Then Boucher showed up for training camp, and Smythe was shocked to see that he weighed no more than 135 pounds (61 kg). But what Boucher lacked in size, he more than made up for in skill and class. He had an uncanny ability to draw defenders to him and then to thread a perfect pass to one of his line-mates for a score. He was also one of the great gentlemen of hockey. In an era of hard-nosed play, Boucher got into only one fight during his 14-year Hall of Fame career in the NHL— and that occurred in his very first game in a Rangers sweater, when he stood up to a challenge from Montreal Maroons forward Merlyn "Bad Bill" Phillips. Starting in 1928, Boucher was awarded the Lady Byng Trophy for sportsmanship seven times in an eight-year span. Finally, in 1935, the league decided to give the trophy permanently to Boucher and to commission a new one for later honorees.

Flopping and scrambling, Patrick allowed only one goal, and the Rangers triumphed 2–1 in overtime. The next game, Joe Miller took over in goal, and the Rangers won two of the next three games to capture the Stanley Cup. Amazingly, Tex's Rangers were champions of the 10-team NHL in only their second year of existence.

The Rangers continued to play high-caliber hockey over the next few seasons, reaching the Cup Finals again in both 1929 and 1932, though they failed to win a title either year. The Blueshirts made it to the Finals again in 1933. This time, they came out on top, as Bill Cook netted an overtime goal in Game 4 to topple the Toronto Maple Leafs and earn New York its second Stanley Cup.

The original Rangers were starting to age, however, and the team began sliding in the standings. In 1935–36, after the Blueshirts failed to qualify for

Vic Hadfield WING

When Vic Hadfield first joined the Rangers in 1961, the club was mired near the bottom of the league standings. By the time he finished his career in New York, the team was a consistent Stanley Cup contender. Aggressive on both offense and defense, Hadfield was feared by opponents for his powerful slap shot and his devastating forechecking. On the offensive end of the ice, he would plant himself near the opponents' goal and hold his position to bang in any loose puck that came his way. In 1971–72, he became the first Rangers player ever to score 50 goals in a season.

RANGERS SEASONS: 1961–78
HEIGHT: 5-9 (175 cm)
WEIGHT: 175 (79 kg)

- 323 career goals
- 389 career assists
- 2-time All-Star
- Led NHL in penalty minutes (151) in 1963–64

The Rangers earned the adoration of New York—and the congratulations of mayor Jimmy Walker—by bringing the Stanley Cup home in 1928.

the playoffs for the first time, Lester Patrick began rebuilding the roster. He started with two of his own sons, Lynn (a wing) and Muzz (a defenseman), and added wings Brian Hextall and Phil Watson and goaltender Dave Kerr.

The "new" Rangers finished a close second to the Boston Bruins in 1939–40, thanks in large part to Kerr, who won the Vezina Trophy as the league's top goalie. In the postseason, New York eliminated Boston in the semifinals and then defeated Toronto again in the Finals to capture its third Stanley Cup. New York fans were confident that their young stars would bring home many more championships. They would never have believed that it would take more than half a century for the Rangers to again hoist the Cup.

"Call them pros, call them mercenaries— but in fact they are just grown-up kids who have learned on the frozen creek or flooded corner lot that hockey is the greatest thrill of all."

NEW YORK COACH LESTER PATRICK

16

RANGERS

AFTER WINNING THEIR THIRD STANLEY CUP in 1940, the Rangers went through a 54-year championship drought. The club made the playoffs 31 times in that period and even reached the Finals in 1950, 1972, and 1979 but kept falling short of another title. Some fans believed that an evil spell had been cast on the team—the Curse of 1940. Two events were cited as the possible origin of the curse. The first occurred during the 1940–41 season, when the mortgage on Madison Square Garden was paid off and team management decided to burn the mortgage papers in the bowl of the Stanley Cup. Since the Cup is considered sacred by many hockey fans, the mortgage burning may have offended an important hockey spirit. Another source of the curse may have been Mervyn "Red" Dutton, coach and general manager of the New York Amerks. In 1942, Rangers management decided not to renew the lease of the Amerks to play in the Garden, and the club went out of business. A bitter Dutton declared that the Rangers would never win another Cup while he was alive. He died in 1987, at the age of 88. Seven years later, the Rangers finally won the Cup.

DOWN DECADES

AFTER THE 1940 CHAMPIONSHIP, THE Rangers rapidly declined. Canada and the United States entered World War II, and the team lost most of its stars to the armed forces. Things got so bad that Lester Patrick considered shutting down operations after the Rangers won just 6 of their 50 games in 1943–44. The club made the playoffs only once more during the 1940s. The offense, led by centers Buddy O'Connor, Ab DeMarco, and Edgar Laprade, continued to excite New York fans, but the team could not score often enough to offset its poor defense and goaltending.

Center Edgar Laprade (right), shown here playing in an NHL All-Star Game, was one of few bright spots in New York during the disappointing 1940s.

The team's goaltending improved significantly when Chuck Rayner took over in the nets in 1945–46. Rayner led the Rangers all the way to the Stanley Cup Finals in 1950 and was awarded the Hart Trophy as the league's Most Valuable Player (MVP) that year. The aggressive Rayner was only the second goalie ever to receive the honor.

The Rangers surprised most experts by simply making the playoffs in 1950. Then they achieved the truly improbable when they knocked off the heavily favored Montreal Canadiens in the opening round to earn a berth in the Cup Finals against the powerful Detroit Red Wings. The Blueshirts won three of the first five games against Detroit and needed one more victory for their first title in a decade. But they failed to hold third-period leads in both Games 6 and 7, losing the final contest and the Cup on a heartbreaking, double-overtime goal by Detroit wing Pete Babando. Some New York fans began to mutter of a curse holding their beloved Rangers back.

Rod Gilbert WING

Rod Gilbert was called up for one game in New York in March 1961 and feared he might never return. In a minor-league game a few nights later, he skated over a piece of debris and broke his back. Gilbert went through a painful recovery period, but he felt the injury made him a better player. "I could never take anything for granted after that," he said. Gilbert rejoined the Rangers before the 1962–63 season and played 16 outstanding years in New York, retiring as the team's all-time leading scorer and holder of 20 other team offensive records.

RANGERS SEASONS: 1961–78
HEIGHT: 5-9 (175 cm)
WEIGHT: 175 (79 kg)

- 406 career goals
- 1976 Masterson Trophy winner (for dedication to hockey)
- 8-time All-Star
- Hockey Hall of Fame inductee (1982)

The inspired play of goalie Chuck Rayner carried an otherwise mediocre 1949–50 Rangers team all the way to the Stanley Cup Finals.

After their near miss in 1950, the Rangers consistently finished near the bottom of the six-team league for the next 16 years. The club went through a long succession of general managers, coaches, and players in unfulfilled hopes of finding a winning combination.

"There's a lot of luck in being a goalie. Sometimes things just go your way, and sometimes you couldn't even stop a basketball."

NEW YORK GOALIE GUMP WORSLEY

Three all-time Rangers favorites skated the New York ice during this period: goalie Lorne "Gump" Worsley and wings Camille Henry and Andy Bathgate. New York fans loved Worsley's outgoing personality and his toughness; he routinely faced 40 to 50 shots a night without a mask. The small (5-foot-9 [175 cm] and 150 pounds [68 kg]) Henry, who was given the nickname "Camille the Eel" because of his elusiveness on the ice, was the team's best power-play performer. Bathgate, a future Hall-of-Famer, had a lightning-fast wrist shot. In 1958–59, he became the first 40-goal scorer in team history and was named league MVP even though the Rangers didn't make the playoffs that year.

Despite the presence of these talented players, the Rangers continued to flounder. Then their fortunes began to rise again when Emile Francis took over as general manager in 1964 and as coach the following year. One of his first moves was to put wings Rod Gilbert and Vic Hadfield alongside center Jean Ratelle. The line clicked and became one of the top scoring trios in the NHL.

The "GAG Line" of Vic Hadfield (top), Rod Gilbert (left), and Jean Ratelle (bottom) thrilled Madison Square Garden crowds in the 1960s.

Sportswriters dubbed the trio the "GAG Line" (suggesting that the trio scored at least one "goal-a-game"). Gilbert and Ratelle were friends from childhood and had played together in junior hockey. Adding Ratelle to the pair seemed to bring out the best in all three men. "Jean and I knew each other's moves so well, we didn't even have to look," said Gilbert. "We needed someone who could do some of the dirty work in the corners and position himself in front of the net without being pushed around. Vic Hadfield was the perfect complement for us."

With the GAG Line providing the offensive punch and young goaltender Eddie Giacomin and All-Star defenseman Brad Park shoring up the defense, the Rangers rose in the standings by the late 1960s and seemed poised to reenter the ranks of the contenders.

"We get nose jobs all the time in the NHL, and we don't even have to go to the hospital."

NEW YORK DEFENSEMAN BRAD PARK

24

RANGERS

Bathgate's Clutch Goal

DURING THE 1950S AND EARLY '60S, THE Rangers often had difficulty qualifying for the postseason. So the pressure was on when they squared off against the Detroit Red Wings at Madison Square Garden on March 14, 1962, with the last playoff spot at stake. The score was tied 2–2 late in the third period when Rangers wing Dean Prentice darted toward the Detroit goal ahead of the defenders. Red Wings goalie Hank Bassen illegally slid his stick across the ice to stop the breakaway. The Rangers were properly awarded a penalty shot, but the referee mistakenly pointed to New York star forward Andy Bathgate to take the shot. The Rangers were thrilled since Bathgate was a far more consistent scorer than Prentice. Bathgate skated methodically toward Bassen "like a mongoose approaching a cobra," according to one reporter. He faked to his left, shifted right, and then sent a backhand shot high into the net for the winning goal. The Garden crowd went crazy, and Bathgate's teammates mobbed him at center ice. "That penalty shot was one of the real highlights of my career," said the future Hall-of-Famer. Rangers fans later voted Bathgate's goal one of the top 10 moments in team history.

ANNUAL DISAPPOINTMENTS

DESPITE THEIR CONSIDERABLE TALENT LEVEL, Francis's Rangers clubs never managed to fulfill expectations. They reached the playoffs each season between 1967 and 1975 but were quickly eliminated year after year. The low point came in 1975, when the Rangers' hated rivals, the crosstown New York Islanders, knocked them out in the first round. "That summer of '75, we got it from everybody," center Pete Stemkowski recalled. "That was the beginning of the Islanders and the beginning of the end of us."

A quietly outstanding center known for his defense and surprising physical strength, Walt Tkaczuk spent all 14 of his NHL seasons in New York.

The team went into another decline until Fred Shero was brought in as coach and general manager before the 1978–79 season. In his first year in New York, Shero, who had led the Philadelphia Flyers to Cup championships in 1974 and 1975, guided the Rangers all the way to the Cup Finals behind the scoring of centers Phil Esposito and Walt Tkaczuk and the goaltending of John Davidson.

As the Rangers made their postseason charge in 1979, everything in New York—from Yankees and Mets baseball games, to operas and concerts, to art and fashion shows, even to Wall Street stock transactions—took a back seat to what was transpiring on the ice at Madison Square Garden. The Rangers were front-page news, rousing hopes that *this* might finally be the year they would end the Stanley Cup drought.

Brad Park DEFENSEMAN

Brad Park spent most of his career as the second-best defenseman in the NHL. During the 1970s, he was generally ranked just behind the great Bobby Orr of the Boston Bruins and was runner-up to Orr four times for the Norris Trophy as the NHL's top defenseman. In the 1980s, he was ranked number two behind Denis Potvin of the New York Islanders. Park was known for both his devastating hip checks, which could slow down any opponent, and his outstanding passing and shooting ability. In 1998, *The Hockey News* included Park in its list of the 50 greatest NHL players of all time.

RANGERS SEASONS: 1968–76
HEIGHT: 6-0 (183 cm)
WEIGHT: 200 (91 kg)

- 213 career goals
- 683 career assists
- 9-time All-Star
- Hockey Hall of Fame inductee (1988)

One of the NHL's most colorful personalities, Phil Esposito remained with New York as an assistant coach and then television analyst after his playing days.

The Rangers demolished the Los Angeles Kings in the first round and whipped Shero's old team, the Flyers, in the second round. That set up a "Battle of New York" against the Islanders for the Campbell Conference championship (the league had been split into the Wales and Campbell Conferences in 1974). "When we won against Los Angeles, nobody really noticed," recalled Davidson, the team's biggest hero during the postseason run. "But when we got it going against the Flyers, that's when the fans started getting into it. Then we faced the Islanders, and every game was a war, a flat-out war. Just great hockey. There was so much emotion on each side."

The Rangers won the war in six games to earn a berth in the Finals against the Montreal Canadiens. Rangers fans dared to believe that the curse would be broken, but they were wrong. The Rangers opened the Finals in fine style, winning Game 1 by a 4–1 score. But New York turned somber as the Canadiens then won the next four games.

The Rangers Family

Bill (left) and Bun Cook (right)

DURING THE LATE 1970S AND EARLY '80S, the Maloney brothers, Dave and Don, were standouts for the Rangers. Older brother Dave, a defenseman, joined the Blueshirts in 1975 at age 20 and became the youngest team captain in franchise history three seasons later. He soon welcomed his younger brother to town, and Don quickly earned a starting role as a high-scoring left wing. The pair played key roles in the Rangers' drive to the Stanley Cup Finals in 1979, and Don later served for many years as the team's assistant general manager. The Maloney brothers continued a long tradition of family members playing for the Rangers. The very first Rangers club featured talented forwards Bill and Bun Cook, and a few years later, Lester Patrick signed up two of his sons, Lynn and Muzz, along with forwards Mac and Neil Colville, as he rebuilt the team in the 1930s. The younger Patricks would each later coach the Rangers, carrying on their father's legacy. Other Blueshirts brothers have included defenseman Gus and center Bill Kyle in the early 1950s, centers Brian and Ray Cullen in the '60s, Gilles and Norm Gratton (at goalie and wing respectively) in the '70s, and forwards Peter and Chris Ferraro in the '90s.

GEARING UP AGAIN

THE HEARTBREAK THAT RANGERS FANS FELT after the 1979 loss was compounded over the next few years, as the Islanders won four straight Stanley Cups in the early 1980s. Suddenly, the Rangers were the second-fiddle hockey team in New York. To rub it in, Islanders fans began chanting "1940! 1940!" whenever the two teams met—a reminder of the last time the Rangers had captured the Cup.

Rangers management tried several different coaches and general managers in an effort to build a consistent winner. The moves didn't result in a championship, but the players who appeared on the Garden's ice in the 1980s—including high-speed center Ron Duguay, brothers Don (at wing) and Dave Maloney (on defense), and spirited goaltender John "Beezer" Vanbiesbrouck—earned loud cheers from the Rangers faithful.

With his long hair, good looks, and swift skating, Ron Duguay was a New York fan favorite for six seasons in the late 1970s and early '80s.

In 1989, Neil Smith, who had helped build a strong minor-league system for the Detroit Red Wings, took over as Rangers general manager and established a new, winning atmosphere. Among Smith's most significant moves were increasing ice time for high-scoring defenseman Brian Leetch, bringing up acrobatic goalie Mike Richter from the minor leagues, and engineering a trade with the Edmonton Oilers before the 1991–92 season for superstar center Mark Messier, who had helped the Oilers win five world championships in the late 1980s and 1990. Led by their new captain, the Rangers earned the 1992 Presidents' Trophy with the best overall record in the league during the regular season (50–25–5), while Messier himself was awarded the Hart Trophy. Still, the team came up short again in the postseason, losing to the Pittsburgh Penguins in a second-round upset.

Brian Leetch DEFENSEMAN

During the 1990s, the Rangers relied on Brian Leetch to both energize their defense and play key roles in the club's offensive attack and power play. Leetch was an extremely fast skater and one of the top passing defensemen of all time. "He was a defensive version of Wayne Gretzky," said teammate Mike Richter. "Brian was talented enough to elevate everybody else's game." In the 1994 playoffs, Leetch scored 34 points in 23 postseason games—the second-highest one-season total ever by a defenseman—to lead the Rangers to the NHL championship. He played in nine All-Star games and starred on three U.S. Olympic squads..

RANGERS SEASONS: 1987–2004
HEIGHT: 6-0 (183 cm)
WEIGHT: 185 (84 kg)

- 781 career assists
- 1989 Calder Trophy winner (as Rookie of the Year)
- 2-time Norris Trophy winner (as best defenseman)
- 1994 Conn Smythe Trophy winner (as playoffs MVP)

Although he was a powerful skater and a great stick-handler, what truly made Mark Messier special was his inspirational on-ice leadership.

After a disastrous 1992–93 season, Smith hired Mike Keenan as coach to whip the team into championship shape. Keenan was known as "Iron Mike" for his no-nonsense personality and demanding coaching style. "I did a few extra sit-ups the day I heard that Mike Keenan was coming here as coach," said Richter. Keenan's style of play was based on a swarming pursuit of the puck and hard-nosed pressure on offense. The players struggled at first to learn the new system, but by midseason, the club was cruising at the top of the Eastern Conference's Patrick Division (the league had been re-split into Eastern and Western Conferences in 1993). New York finished the year with a team-record 52 wins.

This time, the Rangers would not be stopped in the postseason. They swept the hated Islanders in the first round, dispatched the Washington Capitals in round two, and defeated the New Jersey Devils in a thrilling, seven-game battle in the Eastern Conference Finals to reach the Cup Finals against the upstart Vancouver Canucks.

"New York is a great place to play because of the fans. You almost expect to have 100 fans around your car every night. I can't imagine playing somewhere where there isn't that attention."

NEW YORK DEFENSEMAN BRIAN LEETCH

Mike Keenan led New York to the Stanley Cup in his only season there (1993–94) but resigned weeks later after arguing with team management.

The Rangers won three of the first four games against Vancouver and were prepared to close out the series at home in Game 5. "Tonight's the Night!" proclaimed New York newspaper headlines. But it wasn't. The Canucks fought back to win Games 5 and 6 and force a Game 7 showdown in the Garden. Both fearful and hopeful, Garden fans roared their support for the Rangers throughout the final contest, and their faith was rewarded with a 3–2 triumph. "People talked about curses and ghosts and goblins," said an ecstatic Messier as he carried the Cup around the ice. "In New York, it's been 54 years of frustration. The toughest challenge in professional sports was to come here and try to win a championship. But we did it."

"Gone are the days when people look past the New York Rangers. In the past, there were years with the Rangers when the only lure for free agents to come to New York was the money. Now, I think hockey players have seen how much fun it is to play here."

NEW YORK WING BRENDAN SHANAHAN

The Captain's Guarantee

THE RANGERS WERE ABSOLUTELY CERTAIN they were going to win the Stanley Cup in 1994. Then they ran into the New Jersey Devils in the Eastern Conference Finals, and the un-expected began to happen. The Devils cap-tured Game 1 in double overtime to take the series lead, and the teams split the next four games. Suddenly, the Blueshirts were just one game from elimination. That's when Rangers captain Mark Messier made New York sports history. Just as Joe Namath, the quarterback of the New York Jets, had guaranteed a victory in Super Bowl III against the Baltimore Colts,

Messier made his own promise to New York fans before Game 6: "We know we have to win it; we can win it; and we're going to win it!" Messier declared. The Devils weren't im-pressed, however. They jumped out to a 2–0 lead and were cruising toward victory. Then Messier took over, setting up winger Alexei Kovalev for one goal near the end of the sec-ond period and scoring three straight goals himself in the third period to secure the win. The Captain had kept his promise, paving the way for the Rangers to capture the conference crown and win the Cup two weeks later.

of new stars such as winger Jaromir Jagr, defenseman Michal Rozsival, and rookie goaltender Henrik Lundqvist. In 2006–07, veteran winger Brendan Shanahan signed on as a free agent and helped the team become a serious contender in the Eastern Conference once again.

After going on a late-season run to qualify for the 2007 playoffs, the Rangers swept the Atlanta Thrashers in the first round and then battled the top-seeded Buffalo Sabres through six exciting contests before finally falling. As the players left the Madison Square Garden ice after Game 6, they were warmed by a lengthy standing ovation from the appreciative New York fans. "We've turned the corner as a franchise," Shanahan said.

For more than 80 years, the Rangers have brought a combination of excitement and heartache to their legion of fans in New York—not to mention a roster of all-time greats such as Rod Gilbert and Brian Leetch. Hockey-crazed New Yorkers believe that their club is finally free of any curses, and they expect a Blueshirt revival in the Big Apple very soon.

"Good players skate to the puck. Great players skate to where the puck is going to be."

NEW YORK CENTER WAYNE GRETZKY

44

RANGERS

A Feud Among Neighbors

PERHAPS NO RIVALRIES IN HOCKEY ARE more consistently intense than those between the Rangers and their two closest neighbors, the New York Islanders and New Jersey Devils. The Rangers have been around a lot longer than either neighbor—the Islanders were founded in 1972, and the Devils moved to New Jersey from Colorado in 1982—and for a time dominated each opponent on the ice and in the New York press. Then the Islanders put together a championship team and captured four straight Stanley Cups in the early 1980s, defeating the Rangers in early rounds of the playoffs in three of those campaigns. Suddenly, Islanders fans began taunting the Rangers with shouts of "1940! 1940!" and games between the two clubs often included spectacular fights. The Devils joined the rivalry seriously during the 1987–88 season. The Rangers and Devils battled down to the wire for the final playoff spot, which New Jersey won with a victory on the last day of the season. The Devils went on to capture three Cups of their own in 1995, 2000, and 2003. Both the Rangers and Islanders enjoyed a resurgence early in the 21st century, joining the Devils among the league's top teams and making the rivalries likely to intensify in the seasons ahead.

Lester Patrick COACH

When Lester Patrick took on the dual roles of coach and general manager of the Rangers in 1926, he also had a third important job to handle. He had to "sell" hockey to New York sports-writers and fans, most of whom were unfamiliar with the sport. Patrick was successful in all three roles. A tall and dapper man, Patrick could be quite intense and demanding. He even put his son Lynn, a future All-Star, through a tough two-week tryout before agreeing to sign him to a contract. The Lester Patrick Trophy, awarded for outstanding contributions to hockey in the U.S., is named for him.

RANGERS SEASONS AS COACH: 1926–39
NHL COACHING RECORD: 281–216–107
STANLEY CUP CHAMPIONSHIPS WITH NEW YORK: 1928, 1933
HOCKEY HALL OF FAME INDUCTEE (1947)

INDEX